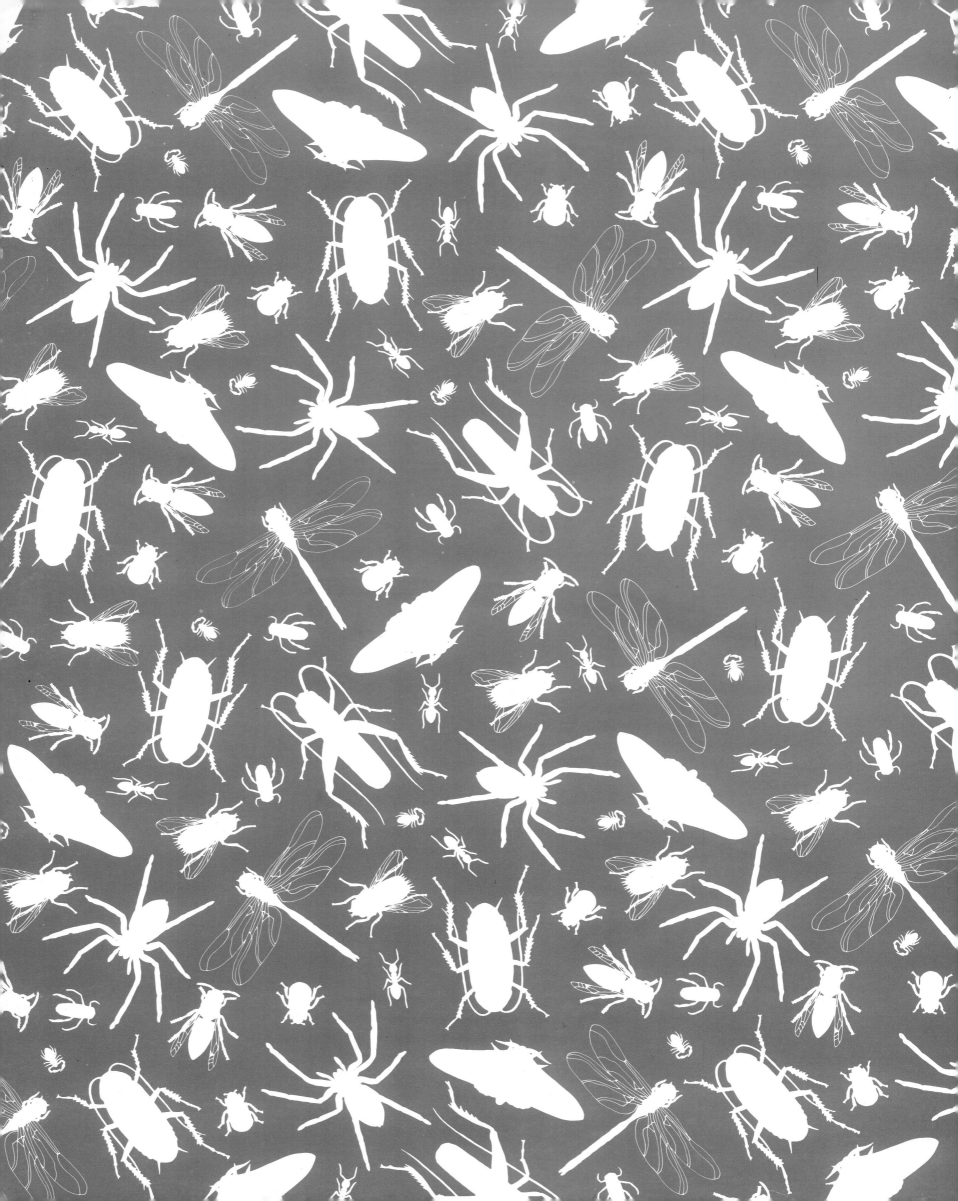

BUGS

BUGS

A closer look at the world's tiny creatures

Written by
Jinny Johnson

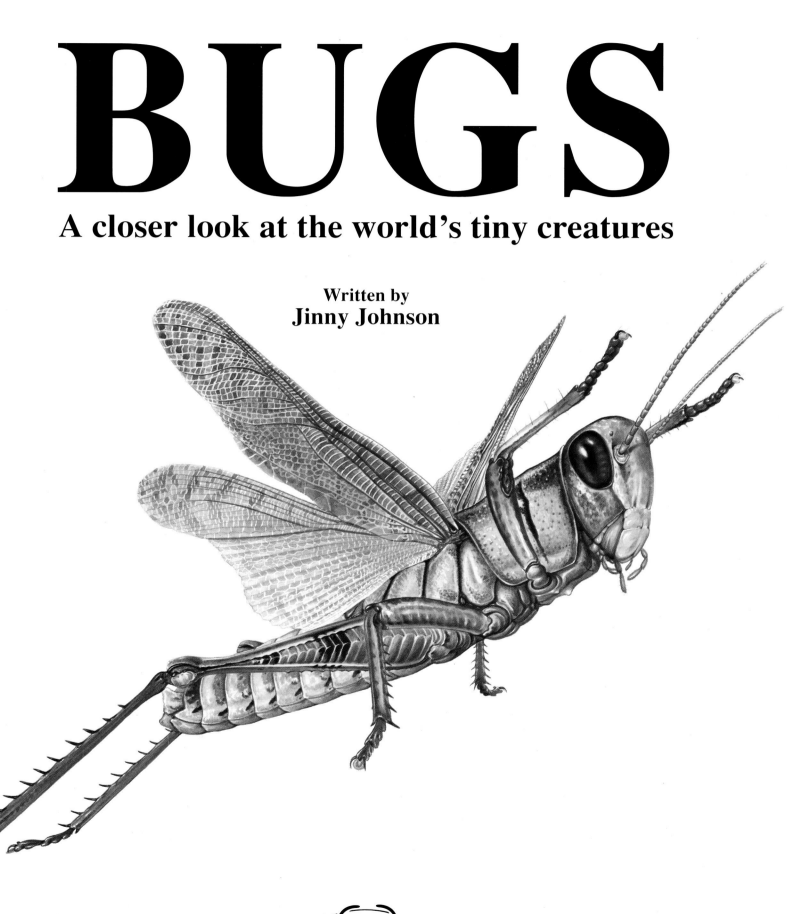

BIG FACE
B O O K S™

This Edition Exclusive to

Project Editor: Ann Kay
Designers: Ralph Pitchford, John Kelly
Consultant: Dr. Philip Whitfield
Researchers: Jazz Wilson, Liz Ferguson, Liz Hirst

Marshall Editions would like to thank the following artists for illustrating this book:

Richard Coombes 14–15, 42–43
Joanne Cowne 11, 15tr, 16–17, 18–19, 20–21, 26–27, 36–37, 38–39, 42tl
Adrian Lascom (Garden Studio) 10
Bernard Robinson 8–9, 12–13
Colin Woolf (Linda Rogers Associates) 22–23, 24–25, 28–29, 30–31, 32–33, 34–35, 40–41

Cover artwork: **Sharon McCausland**
Cover designer: **Michael Harnden**

Originated by Master Image, Singapore
Printed in China

Library of Congress Cataloging in Publication Data

Johnson, Jinny.
    Bugs : a closer look at the world's tiny creatures / writtten by Jinny Johnson.
        p.   cm.
  Includes   index.
  ISBN 1-55280-270-1
  1. Insects—Juvenile literature. 2. Spiders—Juvenile literature.
3. Scorpions—Juvenile literature. [1. Insects. 2. Spiders.
3. Scorpions.]   I. Title.
QL467.2.J63 1995
595.7—dc20   94-35361
                                                   CIP
                                                   AC

10 9 8 7 6 5 4 3 2 1

CONTENTS

MANTIDS

Some of the fiercest hunters in the insect world are the mantids. Their strong front legs shoot out toward prey at the speed of lightning and rarely miss. Daytime hunters, mantids live on trees and shrubs and feed mostly on spiders and insects—including other mantids.

There are about 1,800 kinds of mantids, most living in warm parts of the world. The majority have long, slender bodies and triangular heads. Each mantid has six legs: the front pair are hunting tools, and the four thinner legs are used for walking and holding on to twigs and branches.

Staying hidden until ready for attack is an important part of the mantid's hunting technique. Many mantids are green and look much like leaves or grass. Others are colored like tree bark, twigs, or even flowers. This camouflage also helps protect mantids from creatures that prey on them, such as birds and lizards.

Angola mantis
The speckled colors of this mantis merge with the tree bark.

Flower mantis
Well camouflaged to match the pink orchid flower on which it lives, this mantis waits patiently for prey to come near.

Female mantids are usually larger than males. The females are well known for their habit of attacking and even eating males after mating. The male must get away quickly if he is to escape his mate's spiny grasp.

The mantid is a fussy eater. It throws away the legs, wings, and any other parts of its victim that it does not like.

Praying mantis

The habit of holding its front legs together like someone at prayer earned this mantis its common name. Many other mantids are now known as praying mantids. This mantis lives in Europe and North America. It is usually bright green—to blend in with the leaves it lives on.

Large, widely spaced eyes help the mantid pinpoint the position of prey. Its head swivels freely on its neck and, unlike other insects, the mantid can turn its head and look over its shoulder to follow the movements of its victim.

A mantid's mouthparts are very strong—able to crunch through the toughest insect prey.

The front legs of the mantid have large muscles and are much stronger than its other legs. The inside edges of the front legs are lined with sharp spines, which help the mantid to hold on to struggling prey as it feeds.

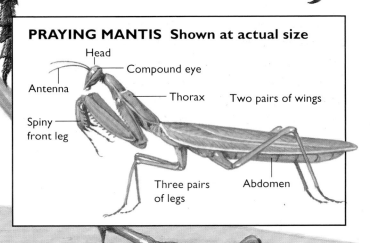

PRAYING MANTIS Shown at actual size

Head

Compound eye

Antenna

Thorax

Two pairs of wings

Spiny front leg

Three pairs of legs

Abdomen

California oak gall wasp
This type of wasp lays her eggs in oak leaves.

Blue-black spider wasp
The spider wasp catches spiders to feed her young.

Giant hornet
Like the yellow jacket, the hornet is a wasp with a powerful sting.

WASPS

Buzzing around a picnic, wasps may seem like a nuisance, but they are really very useful creatures. Wasps feed their young on other insects—often caterpillars and aphids that can do serious harm to various garden and food plants. Without wasps, there would be many more of these pests. Adult wasps like to eat nectar and other sweet things. They have strong jaws, and with these they bite into soft, ripe fruit.

Some types of wasps, such as mud daubers and spider wasps, live alone and make their own nests for their eggs. Many other kinds, including yellow jackets and hornets, live in big groups, which are called colonies. They build their nests from paper, which they make by chewing up tiny pieces of wood to a paper pulp and mixing it with spit in their mouths. Nests are made underground or in bushes or hollow trees.

Wasp colonies do not store food, and all the members of a colony except the queen die in winter. She hibernates, living off her body fat. In spring she lays eggs and starts a new colony.

Black and yellow mud dauber wasp
The female mud dauber lays her eggs in a nest that she makes from balls of damp mud.

Giant ichneumon wasp
Female ichneumon wasps lay their eggs in wood, depositing them on the young of the wood wasp.

Red velvet ant
The velvet ant is a wasp with a painful sting. The female, shown below, does not have wings.

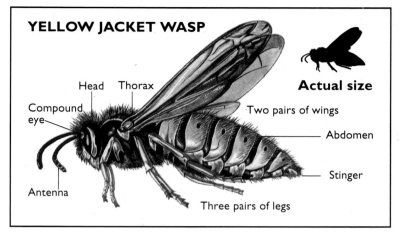

Head   Thorax

Compound
eye

Two pairs of wings

Actual size

Abdomen

Stinger

Antenna

Three pairs of legs

Yellow jacket wasp
There are many kinds of yellow jacket wasps in North America. All have thick, striped bodies. Female yellow jackets lay their eggs in nests that they make underground or beneath fallen logs.

The bright colors of the wasp probably act as a warning to its enemies—keep away or else. When a creature such as a bird attacks a wasp and gets stung, it learns to link the black and yellow stripes with the painful sting. This makes it less likely to attack another wasp.

The wasp's antennae are covered with tiny hairs and are highly sensitive to touch and smell. The antennae may also detect changes in temperature and humidity.

At the end of the body is the stinger. This is a tube with two sharp points, which is linked to a bag of venom. A wasp uses its sting to defend itself against enemies and to kill prey. When the stinger is pushed into a victim, venom flows down through the tube. The wasp can pull out its stinger and use it again.

The scorpion's abdomen has two parts—the wider front part and a long section like a tail with a stinger at the end. When the scorpion attacks its prey, it swings its "tail" forward over its body, bringing the stinger into place.

The last section of the scorpion's "tail" contains a pair of venom-making glands. Venom is forced out of these, into the hollow stinger, and then into the prey.

Desert scorpion
This scorpion lives in the southwestern United States. It is very venomous and preys mostly on small insects. Here it prepares to attack a locust with its stinger.

At the front of the scorpion's body are a pair of pincers, called pedipalps, used for grabbing and holding prey. The food is chewed up with smaller pincerlike jaws, called chelicerae.

SCORPIONS

Whipscorpion
If attacked, this relative of the true scorpion can spray an acidic liquid from the base of its tail.

U sually just a few inches long, scorpions are feared as deadly hunters. They use the venomous stinger at the end of their body to kill prey and to defend themselves. A few kinds of scorpions have venom so strong that it can kill a human, but the sting of most scorpions is no worse than a bee or wasp sting.

Scorpions are not actually insects but relatives of spiders. Like spiders, they have eight legs, while insects have only six. Scorpions live in all the warmer parts of the world, from deserts to rain forests. There are about 1,500 different kinds. The biggest specimens measure up to six inches long.

During the day scorpions stay hidden under stones or logs or deep in underground burrows. At night they come out to hunt for such prey as spiders and insects. The largest scorpions sometimes even attack mice and small lizards. A hunting scorpion grabs its prey in its huge claws. If the prey is large and struggling, the scorpion paralyzes or kills it with its stinger before eating it. Scorpions do have eyes but they cannot see well. They find their prey mostly by their sense of touch, using fine hairs attached to nerves on their body, legs, and pincerlike claws to sense movements.

Windscorpion
Also known as a sun spider, the windscorpion gets its name from its habit of running very fast—like the wind.

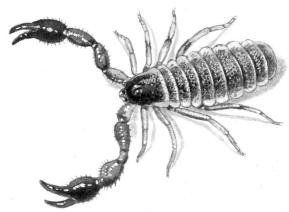

Pseudoscorpion
Only a quarter of an inch long at most, the pseudoscorpion has huge pincers for its size, but no stinger.

Centruroides scorpion
The centruroides scorpion lives in the southern United States. The newborn young climb up onto their mother's back. Here they stay in safety for a few weeks.

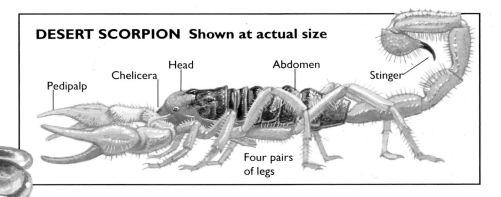

DESERT SCORPION Shown at actual size

Pedipalp
Chelicera
Head
Abdomen
Stinger
Four pairs of legs

13

BEETLES

There are more types of beetles in the world than of any other creature. More than 300,000 species of beetles are known already, and new ones are discovered every year. Beetles live just about everywhere in the world—from small ponds and icy rivers to the driest deserts and the dampest rain forests.

Beetles vary in size from tiny creatures a fraction of an inch long to the Hercules beetle, one of the biggest insects, which is more than six inches in length. But all have a similar body plan, with strong biting mouthparts and a hard protective skeleton on the outside of the body. Most beetles have two pairs of wings. The front ones are made of tough material and form protective wing cases, called elytra, for the delicate back wings. When the beetle is not flying, the back pair are folded under the wing cases. A few kinds of beetles, such as ground beetles, have small back wings or even none at all.

Diving beetle
This lives in water and uses its hind legs as paddles for swimming.

Tiger beetle
Although it is less than an inch long, the tiger beetle is a fierce hunter—like the animal it is named after. It is a fast runner and flier and chases and kills other insects. Each leg ends in a pair of sharp claws that help the beetle catch its prey. Here, the tiger beetle is about to attack an ant.

On the beetle's head are its eyes, a pair of antennae, and the biting jaws used to crush and eat prey. The long antennae, or feelers, help the beetle to search its surroundings by smell, taste, and touch.

14

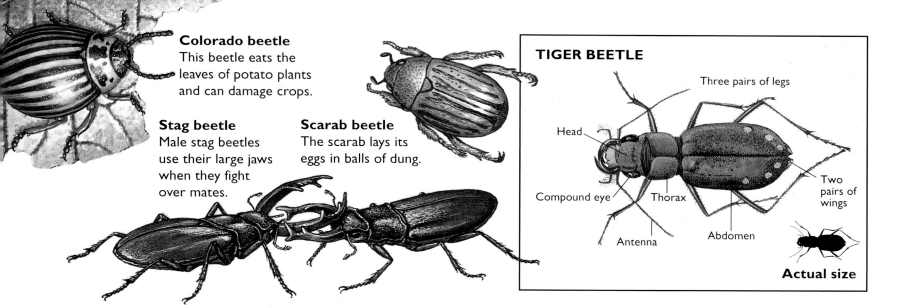

Colorado beetle
This beetle eats the leaves of potato plants and can damage crops.

Stag beetle
Male stag beetles use their large jaws when they fight over mates.

Scarab beetle
The scarab lays its eggs in balls of dung.

TIGER BEETLE

Head

Compound eye

Antenna

Three pairs of legs

Thorax

Abdomen

Two pairs of wings

Actual size

The beetle breathes in a different way from us. Along the sides of its abdomen and thorax are small holes called spiracles. Air enters these holes and travels along fine tubes to all parts of the beetle's body.

Three pairs of long, spiny legs are attached to the beetle's thorax, the middle part of its body. The beetle's wings are also attached to its thorax.

15

CAMOUFLAGE

Insects and spiders are food for all kinds of other creatures, and so they have many different ways of defending themselves. Some are poisonous, and others taste unpleasant. For many, however, the best way to avoid being eaten is to stay well hidden. Some simply tuck themselves under stones or leaves, but others are colored or shaped in a way that helps them to merge into their surroundings. This is called camouflage and makes the insects hard for other creatures to see.

There are insects and spiders that look remarkably like leaves or twigs, and others that are colored like bark or lichen. Some leaflike insects even have irregular edges to their bodies or wings that make them appear to have been nibbled by caterpillars.

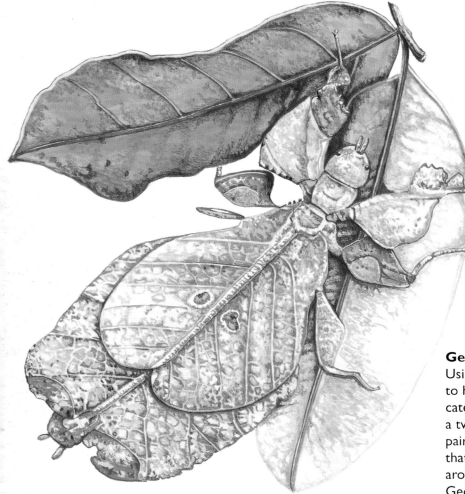

Lichen spider
Mottled colors and tufts of tiny hairs covering its body and legs help keep this spider well hidden on lichen-covered tree bark. If the spider suspects danger is near, it flattens itself even more against the bark and becomes very difficult to see.

Geometrid caterpillar
Using the pair of claspers at the end of its body to hold on to its food plant, the geometrid caterpillar stretches itself out to look like a twig. The caterpillar also has three pairs of legs just behind its head that it uses when moving around the plant. Geometrid caterpillars are between one and two inches long.

Leaf insect
The wings of this insect are leaf shaped and even have veinlike markings. Sitting on a leafy bush, the insect is almost invisible. Its color varies according to the light—it becomes darker at night and paler again by day. Most leaf insects are less than four inches long.

Crab spider

This little spider stays hidden in order to surprise prey. It sits on a flower that more or less matches its own body color and waits for an insect to come and feed on the nectar. It then seizes the insect in its front legs and kills it with a bite, usually to the neck. The venom in the spider's bite paralyzes the victim. The crab spider is only about half an inch long.

Walkingstick

With its slender, brown body, the walkingstick looks like a leafless twig. During the day it clings to a plant, and its long, thin legs sway gently to look as though they are being blown by the breeze. At night it moves around the plant and feeds on leaves. Walkingsticks in North America are about three to six inches long.

Peppered moth

Like most moths, the peppered moth flies at night. During the day it rests on tree trunks, where its speckled colors hide it from birds. In the 1800s, when coal dust and other pollution darkened tree trunks in industrial areas, the moths gradually became darker. Now that this kind of pollution is less of a problem, the moths are again lighter in color. The peppered moth is about one and a half inches wide with its wings fully spread.

Bush katydid

Also known as bush crickets, these insects have wings that look amazingly leaflike and are usually colored to merge with the plants that they eat. There are also some kinds of bush katydid that resemble dead leaves or are colored like lichen or bark. Bush katydids are one and a half to two and a half inches long.

BECOMING A MOTH
As soon as a caterpillar hatches from the egg, it uses all of its energy to feed and grow. Its body gets bigger and bigger, growing so fast that it has to shed its skin several times.

Polyphemus moth

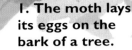

1. The moth lays its eggs on the bark of a tree.

2. The caterpillar hatches out and starts to feed.

3. The adult caterpillar becomes a pupa. It stays inside its pupal case while its body changes.

4. Finally, the adult moth comes out of the pupal case.

MOTHS

How can you tell a moth from a butterfly? There are no definite differences, but generally most butterflies are brightly colored, fly in the daytime, and have knobbed antennae on their heads. Moths are often duller in color, fly at night, and have feathery or straight antennae. One other difference is that a butterfly rests with its wings held together over its back while a moth holds its wings flat or curled around its body.

There are more than 200,000 kinds of butterflies and moths. All have tiny scales covering their wings and bodies. These scales are actually tiny flattened hairs and create the colorful patterns seen on the wings of many of these insects.

All butterflies and moths start life as an egg, which hatches into a caterpillar. Caterpillars eat plant leaves and shoots. Most adult butterflies and moths suck nectar from flowers or juice from fruits.

Atlas moth
This is one of the largest of all moths. It has a wingspan of 12 inches.

Ornate tiger moth
The ornate tiger moth gets its name from its striped, furry body.

Luna moth
The caterpillars of the luna moth eat the leaves of trees such as hickory, walnut, and sweet gum.

The moth's antennae are very sensitive to smell as well as touch. Moths can pick up the faintest scents, which a human would not notice, and this sense of smell helps them to find food and mates. Females also use their antennae to help them choose the right food plants on which to lay eggs.

White-lined sphinx moth
The white-lined sphinx, also known as the striped hawk-moth, lives in North America and Europe. Of all butterflies and moths, sphinx moths are among the most powerful fliers. They can even hover like hummingbirds in front of flowers as they feed. Their wings beat so fast that they make a whirring noise.

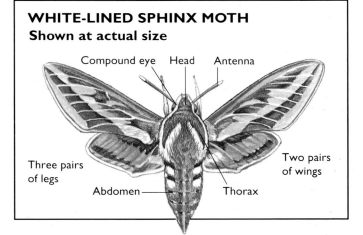

WHITE-LINED SPHINX MOTH
Shown at actual size

Compound eye   Head   Antenna

Three pairs of legs

Two pairs of wings

Abdomen   Thorax

Many kinds of moths have brownish front wings to help keep them hidden when resting during the day. If in danger, a moth may reveal the brighter colored back wings to startle its enemy.

Although most spiders have eight eyes, few have good eyesight. They rely on hairs on their body and legs to sense movement around them. But some spiders, such as jumping spiders and wolf spiders, do have good sight, which makes it much easier for them to spot prey.

Wolf spider

Like the animal it is named after, the wolf spider is a fast-moving, stealthy hunter. Once it has detected the movement of its victim, the wolf spider creeps up on it and then makes a final speedy dash to grab the prey in its strong jaws.

A spider's legs are made up of seven segments. Each leg is tipped with two or three claws. Some spiders also have tiny tufts of hair, helping them to grip on to surfaces as they walk.

A spider bites its prey with the strong jaws, or chelicerae, at the front of its head. On each jaw is a sharp, hinged fang, linked to a venom gland. As the spider bites, venom flows through the fangs. This paralyzes the victim and actually dissolves its body so that the spider can suck it up through its mouth.

SPIDERS

Big or small, spiders are all hunters. Some trap their prey in sticky webs. Others, such as crab spiders, lie hidden or camouflaged, waiting to ambush their victims. And wolf spiders stalk their prey until near enough to pounce. Spiders feed mostly on insects and so help to keep their numbers under control.

Spiders are not insects. An insect has six legs, antennae, and a body divided into three parts. A spider has eight legs, no antennae, and a body divided into two parts. At the front of the spider's head are its chelicerae, a pair of jaws that it uses for grabbing hold of prey, defending itself, and even for digging burrows. A spider also has palps—one on each side of its mouth. These look like small legs but are actually used for sensing and holding. Not all spiders make webs but all can spin silk, which comes from a cluster of short tubes called spinnerets at the rear end of the body.

There are at least 35,000 different species of spiders, and many more are yet to be named. They live in all sorts of areas—from the highest mountains to deep caves, dry deserts, and tropical forests.

Black and yellow argiope spider
This spider spins a web of sticky silk on which to trap its prey.

Black widow spider
The black widow is one of the few kinds of spider that are dangerous to humans.

Red-kneed tarantula
This large spider preys on lizards, mice, and even small birds. Its powerful bite is harmless to humans.

WOLF SPIDER
Shown at actual size

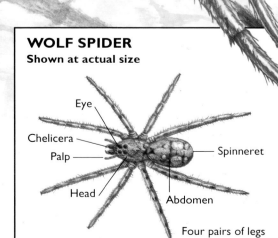

Eye
Chelicera
Palp
Head
Spinneret
Abdomen
Four pairs of legs

Trapdoor spider
Living in a burrow with a hinged door has given this spider its name. When prey wanders by, the spider pops out and drags the victim back into its burrow.

Cat flea

The cat flea lives in the fur of domestic cats all over the world. Pale or reddish brown in color, the cat flea is only a fraction of an inch long. The female cat flea lays up to about 100 eggs at a time—usually in the cat's sleeping place.

The spiny comb on the top of the flea's head helps the flea to hold on to its host. The finer the host's fur, the closer the spines of the comb are. The flea also uses its hooklike claws to hold on to the host's skin.

The flea's bristles and antennae are highly sensitive to the slightest movement and smell from the host. They help the flea to know when a host is coming near so that it can get ready to jump.

Chigoe flea

Most fleas leap onto their hosts to feed and jump off again. But "stick-tight" fleas stay on their hosts all the time. One type, the chigoe, burrows into the host's skin.

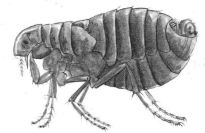

Human flea

These fleas live in human housing— under furniture, in carpets, or anywhere they can easily jump onto humans to feed on their blood.

4. Flea holds its front legs forward to latch on to the host's fur with its hooks.

FLEAS

A flea is able to jump more than 200 times its own body length. If a human could do this, he or she would be able to leap right over the Empire State Building.

Fleas are parasites. This means that they live by feeding on the blood of other creatures, such as cats, dogs, and rats. Fleas need their amazing jumping ability to help them reach the animals they feed on, known as their hosts. Most types of fleas live on a particular type of host animal. There are fleas that live on hedgehogs, rabbits, and even on some birds.

Tiny insects, fleas are mostly under a quarter of an inch long. Their bodies are very flat from side to side, and they have no wings. Hairs on the body and combs of spines on the head help the flea stay lodged safely in the fur or feathers of the host animal—no matter how much it scratches. Once on its host, the flea pierces the skin with its mouthparts and sucks up blood.

Female fleas lay their eggs in the nest or bedding of the host animal. These eggs hatch into larvae, which feed on the undigested droppings of the adult flea or on rotting plant or animal matter in the nest.

3. Flea begins to somersault.

2. Flea continues upward.

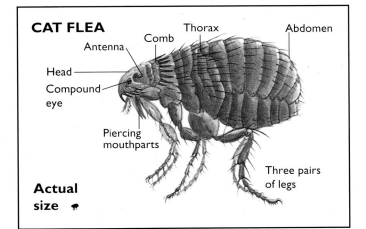

CAT FLEA

Antenna Comb Thorax Abdomen

Head

Compound eye

Piercing mouthparts

Three pairs of legs

Actual size

A MIGHTY LEAP

The "power pack" for the flea's jump is a special part of the body made of resilin, an elastic material. The resilin, which is near the top of the back legs, is kept contracted between jumps. When released, it acts as a spring to catapult the flea upward. The flea somersaults through the air until it reaches its host.

1. Flea takes off.

DRAGONFLIES

B rightly colored, with shimmering, delicate wings, dragonflies are among the most beautiful of all insects. They can also fly fast enough to catch other insects, such as midges and mosquitoes, in the air. With their excellent eyesight, dragonflies can spot tiny prey from many feet away.

Most dragonflies are large insects with long bodies and two pairs of wings. There are two groups: true dragonflies (which include darners, skimmers, and biddies) and damselflies. Most damselflies have thinner bodies than dragonflies and are weaker fliers.

Dragonflies usually live near lakes or rivers and lay their eggs underwater. The eggs hatch into larvae, called nymphs. Like the adults, the nymphs are fierce hunters and catch worms, tadpoles, and even small fish in their strong jaws.

Acrobats in the air, dragonflies are some of the speediest insects. They can fly up to 35 miles an hour, hover while they search for prey, and even fly backward.

There are about 5,000 different kinds of dragonflies living all over the world. They range in size from three fourths of an inch to about five inches long.

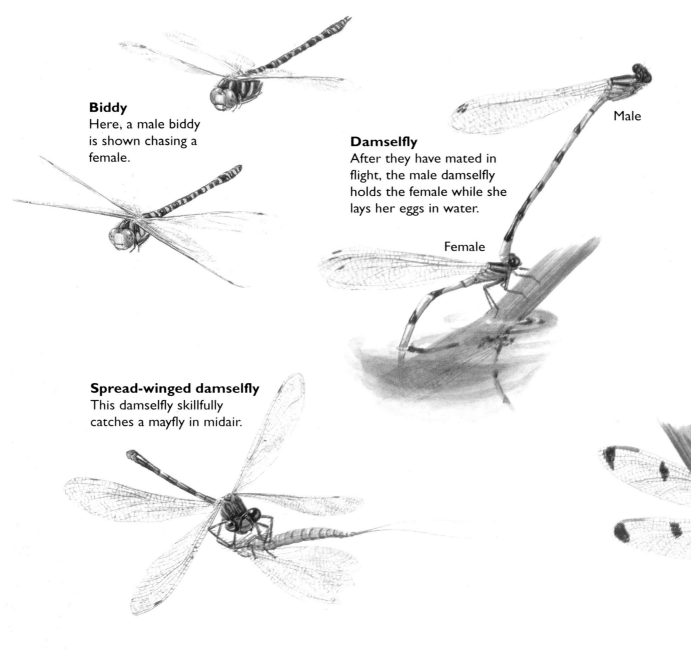

Biddy
Here, a male biddy is shown chasing a female.

Damselfly
After they have mated in flight, the male damselfly holds the female while she lays her eggs in water.

Male

Female

Spread-winged damselfly
This damselfly skillfully catches a mayfly in midair.

Skimmer
The brightly colored skimmer usually lives around swamps.

When hunting, the dragonfly zooms back and forth over water, with its front legs held out ready to grab a smaller insect. After trapping its prey, the dragonfly seizes it in its strong jaws.

Once the dragonfly nymph is fully grown, it crawls out of the water and onto a leaf or rock. The skin on the nymph's back splits open, and the adult dragonfly slowly crawls out. The insect must wait for half an hour or so for its newly unfolded wings to strengthen before flying off, leaving its old skin behind.

Green darner
The green darner is one of the largest and most colorful dragonflies. It is up to three inches long, with wings about four inches across when fully spread. Like most dragonflies, the male darner often has a territory, or specific stretch of land, that he patrols and defends from other dragonflies. He allows his female mates into his territory but chases other males away.

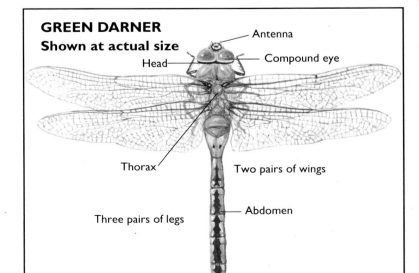

GREEN DARNER
Shown at actual size

Antenna

Compound eye

Head

Thorax

Two pairs of wings

Three pairs of legs

Abdomen

TRAVELERS

Some insects spend their whole lives on one bush. Others travel long distances, sometimes thousands of miles, to find a better climate or good supplies of food. There are insects, such as some kinds of butterflies and moths, that make yearly journeys called migrations. These journeys follow the same routes and are taken at the same time every year. Dragonflies, hover flies, and locusts are among the insects that make less regular journeys to find food or living space.

Migrations are not always by air. Army ants walk for miles in columns of thousands. Caterpillars of the owlet moth family are known as army worms because of their mass marches to find new feeding places.

Convergent ladybug
Swarms of these North American ladybugs fly to sheltered regions to spend the cold winter months. In spring they go back to their feeding areas.

Hover fly
Aerial acrobats, these flies are experts in the air. They dart around in all directions and hover in front of flowers while feeding on pollen and nectar. Huge swarms of these flies sometimes move hundreds of miles to find good feeding areas. Since their young feed on pests such as aphids, their arrival is usually welcomed by gardeners.

Painted lady
In North America some painted lady butterflies go north from Mexico each spring, flying as far as Canada. In Europe painted ladies journey to northern Europe from Africa in spring. No one really understands why the butterflies make these migrations. Some experts think that it may be a way of spreading the population over a wide area.

Army ant
Most ants live in a nest, but army ants stay on the move. In columns of up to 750,000 individuals, they march along, eating almost anything that comes their way. At night they make a living nest out of their own bodies, with their queen and her young in the center.

Monarch butterfly

Millions of these beautiful butterflies travel from northern North America to California and Mexico every fall, flying as far as 2,000 miles to escape the cold northern winter. They spend the winter clinging together in trees. In spring monarch butterflies fly north again. Most of those that return north are probably the young of those that journeyed south the previous fall.

Bean aphid

Aphids are insects that suck the sap of plants. They make journeys that are much shorter than those of the monarch butterfly or desert locust, but just as important. In spring special winged aphids fly off from the plants on which they were born to find new plants to live on.

Desert locust

From time to time, if their numbers increase a lot or food becomes scarce, young locusts grow longer wings and develop brighter colors than the normal nonmigrating locusts. Huge swarms of these locusts fly hundreds of miles in North Africa and the Middle East, destroying crops as they go.

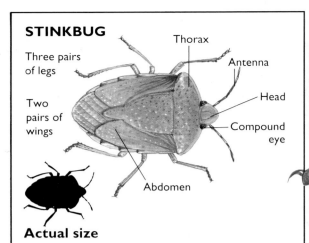

Birds love to eat true bugs, so these insects need to stay hidden if they can. Some true bugs that spend most of their lives on trees are mottled gray and brown to match tree bark. The stinkbug shown here is bright green, making it hard to see when it is feeding on green leaves.

Some true bugs are good mothers. They lay their barrel-shaped eggs in rows on the underside of a leaf. If any danger threatens, the female bug covers the eggs with her own body to protect them.

Stinkbug

Stinkbugs get their name from their habit of spraying foul-smelling liquid at any creature that tries to attack them. The liquid comes from glands on the underside of the insect's body. The stinkbug also has special mouthparts, which are inside a beaklike snout. There are four basic sections to the mouthparts. The outer two have sharp teeth for piercing the surface of a plant or animal in order to get at the sap or body juices. The inner two form a tube for sucking up liquid food.

Back swimmer bug
This type of true bug swims upside down. It lives in ponds and lakes and preys on other insects and tadpoles.

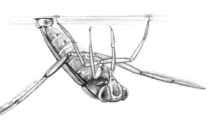

Assassin bug
The assassin bug is a fierce hunter. It stalks its victims and kills them with its sharp, piercing mouthparts.

Plant bug
This bug feeds on plant juices and can damage crops.

Ambush bug
The ambush bug lies in wait for prey and pounces when it comes near.

TRUE BUGS

Anything that crawls is a bug to most people, but "true bug" is the name for insects of a particular group. True bugs are small insects, mostly under an inch long. They have two pairs of wings. The front pair are tough and leathery near the base, and delicate at the tip. These wings can be folded flat over the body, covering the transparent back wings.

True bugs include about 25,000 different species found all over the world—insects such as assassin bugs, plant bugs, and stinkbugs. Most live on land, but some, such as water boatmen and back swimmers, spend their lives in ponds, slow streams, and lakes. These water bugs swim by making rowing movements with their paddlelike legs.

Many true bugs feed on plant sap and fruit juices. Others, such as ambush bugs, attack and kill other insects and feed on their body liquids. And tiny bedbugs live by feeding on the blood of humans and other mammals.

FLIES

Robber fly
This fierce hunter catches other insects.

Deer fly
Deer flies can give painful bites.

Dirty, disease-carrying, and annoying—that's what most people think about flies. But they do have their uses. After bees and wasps, flies are the most important pollinators of flowers. Pollen must be taken from flower to flower so that the flowers are fertilized and produce seeds, and insects such as flies carry pollen as they feed. Flies are also food for lots of other creatures.

There are more than 90,000 species of flies living nearly all over the world, from the hottest deserts to the edges of the polar regions. There are slender, delicate flies, such as midges and dance flies, and thick-bodied kinds, such as blowflies and hover flies.

Unlike other flying insects, flies have just one pair of wings. They also have small balancing organs, called halteres, one on each side of the body. These vibrate and help the fly control its flight as it zooms through the air at high speed.

Most flies have special mouthparts for sucking up liquid foods such as flower nectar, plant sap, and fruit juices. Others, such as houseflies, dung flies, and blowflies, also feed on rotting matter such as dung and dead animals. These flies can carry disease.

Hover fly
Often seen hovering over flowers, the hover fly feeds on nectar.

Dance fly
The male dance fly performs dancing flights to attract mates.

FROM A MAGGOT TO A FLY
Flies usually lay their eggs near some suitable food. The eggs hatch out into wriggling, legless larvae, called maggots. As the maggot grows, it sheds its skin several times. The last larval skin becomes a hard case. Inside, the insect pupates—that is, it turns into an adult fly.

1. Eggs
2. Maggots
3. Pupae
4. Fly emerging from pupal case
5. Adult fly

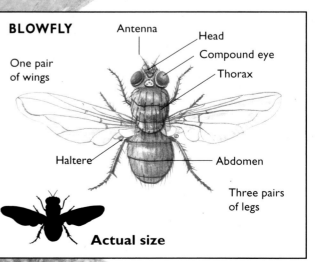

BLOWFLY

Antenna
Head
Compound eye
Thorax
One pair of wings
Haltere
Abdomen
Three pairs of legs

Actual size

30

Blowfly

Blowflies, also known as bluebottles or greenbottles, have thick bodies with a metallic sheen. They lay their eggs on rotting matter, such as dung or meat, or even in the wounds or nostrils of live animals. Adult blowflies are often seen on human food and can carry disease.

The fly moves fast in the air and can hover, fly backward, and turn right around in midair. It has very strong wings, powered by special muscles in the middle of the thorax. Pads and claws on the fly's feet help it land almost anywhere—even upside down on a ceiling.

GRASSHOPPERS

Although they are usually only a couple of inches long, grasshoppers can leap some 200 times their own length. They have long back legs with powerful muscles that help them hop and jump away from enemies such as hungry birds.

Insects such as crickets, katydids, and locusts belong to the grasshopper group. They feed on leaves and grasses and have strong mouthparts for biting and chewing their food.

Besides their jumping ability, grasshoppers are famous for their songs. Usually it is the males that sing—to attract the attention of females. Some kinds of grasshoppers, such as locusts and spur-throated grasshoppers, make buzzing sounds. These sounds are created when the grasshoppers scrape the ridges, which look like rows of tiny pegs, on the inside of their back legs against the thickened edges of their front wings. The scraping action is somewhat like sliding the teeth of a comb across the edge of a card. Other grasshoppers, such as katydids and crickets, rub special hard areas on their front wings together to make their songs.

Mole cricket
The mole cricket spends much of its life burrowing under the ground with its short, strong front legs.

Field cricket
In spring and summer, the field cricket sings day and night.

Carolina locust
This locust can do lots of damage to food crops.

Katydid
The katydid gets its name from its song, which sounds like "katy-did, katy-didn't," chirped over and over again.

When not feeding, grasshoppers stay very still to avoid being noticed by predators. If disturbed, the grasshopper leaps into the air with the help of its strong back legs and flies a short distance until it is safe to drop to the ground again.

32

Most grasshoppers have two pairs of wings. When not in use, the larger, more delicate back wings are folded beneath the narrow, tougher front wings.

Spur-throated grasshopper
This grasshopper is very common in fields and prairies where there are plenty of plants for it to eat. It eats up leaves and flowers so quickly that it can cause great damage to food crops. The female lays her eggs on the ground in fall. They are covered with a sticky substance that dries around them to make a protective case. The eggs hatch the following spring.

Each species of grasshopper has a slightly different song. Grasshoppers have very good hearing, and females are particularly good at recognizing the songs of their own kind. This helps them to know which male grasshopper to mate with. The grasshopper's hearing organs are positioned on the abdomen.

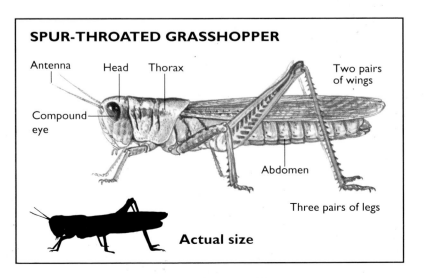

SPUR-THROATED GRASSHOPPER

Antenna — Head — Thorax — Two pairs of wings — Compound eye — Abdomen — Three pairs of legs — **Actual size**

33

ANTS

All ants are tiny—most are well under an inch long. They live in huge, well-organized groups, called colonies. Colonies contain thousands of individuals, and the nest is a maze of chambers and tunnels made underground or in rotting wood.

Most members of an ant colony are female. Each colony includes at least one queen ant, and the queens lay all of the eggs. The workers are also female and do not have wings. Workers cannot lay eggs—they gather food and look after the nest, eggs, and young. Some workers are called soldiers. They have big jaws, and it is their job to defend the colony.

Each colony also contains special male and female ants with wings. In spring or summer, they fly off from the colony to find mates. After mating, the males die. The females (who will now become egg-laying queens) break off their wings and look for a place to start a nest.

As ants scurry around in search of food, they lay scent trails. These are sensed by the antennae of other ants, leading them to food and helping them find their way back to the nest. Each colony has its own special smell. Ants also seem to "talk" to each other by rubbing their antennae together.

Carpenter ant
Carpenter ants make their nests in old buildings, logs, and poles, and they can do a great deal of damage. As with all ants, the queen lays all the eggs for the colony. Here, a worker ant is removing an egg just laid by the queen and will take it to the colony's nursery area.

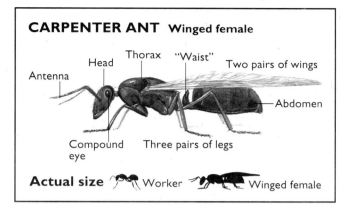
There are thousands of different kinds of ants, but most have slender bodies with a definite "waist" between the thorax and abdomen. Ants also have unusual antennae with an elbowlike bend in the middle.

Fire ant
These ants have a painful bite and sting. They catch other insects to eat and also feed on seeds, fruit, and flowers.

Red ant
The main food of red ants is aphid honeydew, a sweet liquid that comes out of the bodies of tiny bugs called aphids. Red ants also feed on flower nectar.

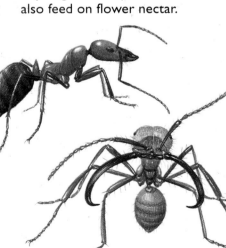

Leaf-cutting ant
These ants cut pieces of leaves and carry them back to their nest to make "gardens" on which fungi grow. The ants feed on the fungi.

Harvester ant
This ant gets its name from its habit of feeding on seeds and grain crops.

Army ant
Huge troops of army ants march together through forests. Using their big, strong jaws, they attack any insects or small creatures, such as worms, in their path.

BUILDERS

Some of the most impressive structures in the animal world are built by insects such as wasps, bees, ants, and termites. Termites make towering mounds on the ground or ball-shaped nests in trees. Ants build huge underground cities, and bees and wasps make complex nests on branches or buildings. Most of these expert builders are social insects. They live in large groups, or colonies, and there are always plenty of individuals to do the work of making the nest.

In these amazing homes, the insects keep their eggs and young warm and sheltered from the outside world and its dangers. Some of these insects, such as honeybees and many ants and termites, also store food there for use in winter.

Workers building the nest with spit and soil

Queen laying eggs

Workers

Termite
These small, soft-bodied insects make the most spectacular of all insect nests. The huge mounds built by some African and Australian termites can be more than 16 feet tall and are made of soil mixed with the termites' spit. Tall chimneys inside the mound let air in and out and help keep the temperature even. The nest itself is a maze of chambers and tunnels. There are areas for food storage, for eggs and young, and a royal chamber where the queen, the head of the colony, lives. In special "garden" chambers the termites grow fungi, similar to tiny mushrooms, to eat. More than a million termites—most of them workers—live together in a large nest.

Workers carrying eggs to special chambers

Chimney

Workers collecting fungi

Mound on tree

Umbrella-shaped mound

Workers bringing food into nest

Wood ant

All ants live in huge colonies. They usually make moundlike nests that may be several feet high. The nest contains chambers both above and below ground and may be built around an old tree stump. Ants use soil and plant material such as leaves, twigs, and grass to build a series of tiny chambers supported by columns and walls. Tunnels link the chambers and provide entrances and exits for the nest. The ants keep the temperature inside the nest just right by piling plant material onto the outside of the mound to make the nest warmer, or removing it to cool the nest down.

Worker ant

Workers tending eggs and pupae in nest chambers

Ant lion

Adult ant lions are winged insects a little like damselflies. The name really applies to the young, or larvae, which are fierce hunters of ants and other insects, and which build traps to catch prey. Soon after it emerges from the egg, the ant lion larva makes a pit in the sand. It sits half-buried at the bottom, waiting for prey to fall down the sloping sides. The ant lion then attacks its victim with its strong jaws.

Paper wasp

The female paper wasp builds her nest with a papery material that she makes from chewed wood mixed with her spit. The nest hangs from a branch or from the eaves of a building. Unlike other wasps, she does not make an outside covering for the nest but leaves the honeycomb-like cells open. She lays her eggs in the cells, and more females join her to help feed the young with other insects. A paper wasp nest usually contains about 20 wasps.

Ant lion larva

37

BEES

Strict vegetarians, bees are unlike wasps in that they do not catch other insects to eat or to feed to their young. All bees feed on pollen and nectar, which they get from flowers. They have long tongues for sucking up nectar, and most have special features, such as stiff hairs on their legs, for carrying pollen back to their nests.

There are about 22,000 species of bees. Some kinds, such as leaf-cutter bees, live alone and make their own nests for their young. Others, such as honeybees and bumblebees, are social creatures, living together in huge colonies that contain as many as 80,000 bees. Each colony includes one queen, tens of thousands of worker bees (which are female), and some male drones. The queen is the head of the colony and lays all the eggs—as many as 1,500 in a day. Male drones mate with new queens, who start new colonies or take over when the old queen dies.

Leaf-cutter bee
This bee has earned its name by cutting pieces of leaf to build and line its nest.

Bumblebee
The bumblebee usually makes its nest underground.

Plasterer bee
The walls of this bee's underground burrow are lined with a liquid from the bee's own body. The liquid dries to make a waterproof covering that helps keep the nest dry.

California carpenter bee
The female bee digs a tunnel-like nest in wood. She makes a line of separate cells inside the tunnel, fills them with pollen food stores, and lays one egg in each cell.

BUILDING A NEST
The honeybee builds its nest from wax made in its own body. The nest consists of sheets, called combs, made up of thousands of hexagonal (six-sided) cells. These hang in a shelter such as a hollow tree. Some cells are for storing food—honey or pollen. Other cells contain eggs or young larval bees.

Worker (female) honeybee

Drone (male) honeybee

Queen honeybee

Honeybees' comb

Honeybee

A worker honeybee lives only six to eight weeks. For the first week of her life a worker cares for the eggs and larvae. Then she helps with the building and cleaning of the nest. Finally, for her last few weeks, the worker becomes a food gatherer.

When the worker bee sucks nectar from a flower, some goes into a storage bag in her body. On returning to the nest, she spews it out. Other workers take the nectar and make it into honey.

WORKER HONEYBEE

Actual size

Head

Thorax

Antenna

Compound eye

Two pairs of wings

Abdomen

Pollen sac

Three pairs of legs

Watch a bee leaving a flower and you may see yellow blobs on its legs. These are full pollen sacs. The bee has a pollen sac—a groove lined with stiff hairs—on each of its back legs. When the bee visits a flower, pollen grains from the flower cling to the hairs on its body and front legs. The bee scrapes the pollen onto the sacs to carry back to the nest.

39

COCKROACHES

Tough survivors, cockroaches can last for a month without water and for three months without food. They live everywhere except in polar regions. There are burrowing cockroaches that live in the soil and forest-dwelling kinds that hide under bark and leaves. Best known of all, however, are the few types that live in human homes and other buildings.

Cockroaches have long legs and flattened bodies—an ideal shape for squeezing into cracks and between floorboards. Most have two pairs of wings. The front pair are strong and leathery and can be folded over the delicate back wings to protect them. But cockroaches usually fly only short distances and tend to rely more on fast running to escape from danger.

During the day cockroaches stay hidden, but at night they come out to look for food. In the wild, cockroaches feed mostly on plants, but they also eat dead insects and animal droppings. In buildings, they feed on anything they can find, including garbage.

Harlequin cockroach
This patterned cockroach lives in Central American forests.

Oriental cockroach
A serious pest worldwide, the oriental cockroach is often found in basements and cellars.

German cockroach
This cockroach actually lives all over the world, usually indoors, in houses, stores, and restaurants.

Cockroaches are among the most ancient of all insects. They first lived more than 350 million years ago—long before the dinosaurs—and have changed little since then.

1. Female cockroach laying egg case.

2. Young cockroaches emerging from egg case.

3. Young cockroach

BEARING YOUNG

The female cockroach lays her eggs in a tough, purse-shaped container, which keeps the eggs safe until they hatch.

The cockroach has strong mouthparts for biting and chewing all kinds of food. The head also carries two very long and sensitive antennae.

American cockroach

Common in buildings and warehouses all over North America, this cockroach has spread to many other parts of the world. Like rats, these cockroaches are pests. They often spoil food when they walk over it with feet that are dirty from drains and sewers.

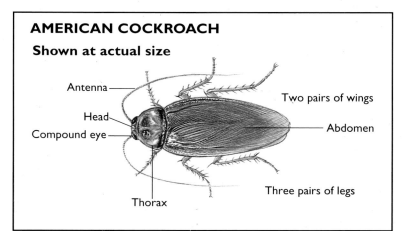

AMERICAN COCKROACH

Shown at actual size

Antenna

Head

Compound eye

Thorax

Two pairs of wings

Abdomen

Three pairs of legs

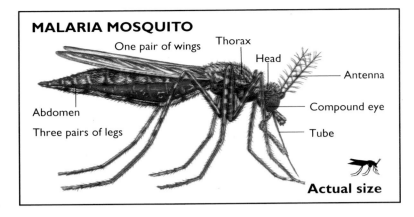

MALARIA MOSQUITO

One pair of wings

Thorax

Head

Antenna

Compound eye

Abdomen

Three pairs of legs

Tube

Actual size

Malaria mosquito

The mosquito shown here often carries the tiny parasites that cause a serious illness called malaria. These parasites enter the victim's blood as the mosquito bites. Malaria-carrying mosquitoes live in most warm parts of the world, in forest and woodland, and around humans. They need water nearby in which to lay their eggs—even a rain puddle will do.

A female's biting equipment includes a fine, sharp-tipped tube, with a protective cover around it. The tube is hollow, rather like a hypodermic needle. With this, the insect cuts into the victim's skin and feeds on its blood.

The antennae on the female's head are very sensitive to smell. They can pick up the scent of a potential victim hundreds of feet away.

42

A female mosquito's wings can beat an amazing 500 times a second. They move so quickly that all that can be heard is a constant whining hum as the insect flies.

1. Egg

2. Larva

FROM EGG TO ADULT

Mosquitoes lay their eggs in water—in ponds and lakes, for example—where they float on the surface. The eggs hatch into wriggling larvae, which look very different from the adult insects. These larvae feed on tiny creatures in the water. When fully fed, each larva develops into a pupa, which can swim but does not eat. A few days later the skin of the pupa breaks open, and an adult struggles out.

3. Pupa

4. Adult

MOSQUITOES

Only female mosquitoes bite animals, such as humans, and feed on their blood. Male mosquitoes do not bite—flower nectar is their main food. The female has a special tubelike mouth for piercing the skin of victims and sucking up the blood. An ingredient in the mosquito's spit stops the victim's blood from clotting so that it flows easily. The spit also makes the bite itch. In a single meal a female mosquito can take in more than twice her own weight in blood. Her abdomen swells until it looks like a red balloon. Females need the protein they get from blood in order to make their eggs.

Mosquitoes are slender, long-winged flies, and they live in most parts of the world. There are more than 3,000 different kinds of mosquitoes. Some carry tiny parasites in their bodies that cause extremely serious diseases such as malaria and yellow fever. Because they spread such dangerous illnesses as they bite, mosquitoes are among the deadliest of all living creatures.

GLOSSARY

Abdomen
The third part of an insect's body, behind the head and thorax.

Antennae (*singular,* antenna)
A pair of slender, sensitive structures on an insect's head. These "feelers" help an insect to sense things in its surroundings by smell, taste, and touch.

Camouflage
Color or pattern on an insect's body that help it to hide in its surroundings. For example, many insects are colored green to match the leaves they live on.

Cell
A six-sided space in the nest of a bee or wasp that is often used for the storage of food or eggs.

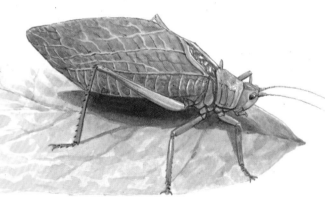

Chamber
Section of a nest of insects such as ants and termites. There are usually separate chambers for purposes such as rearing young and storing food.

Chelicerae (*singular,* chelicera)
Strong jaws at the front of a spider's or scorpion's head. On each jaw is a fang.

Cocoon
A case made of silk that protects the pupa of insects such as moths.

Colony
A large group of insects that live together in a nest. Ants, termites, and some wasps and bees live in colonies.

Compound eye
An eye made up of hundreds of different parts, each with a tiny lens at its surface. Some insects and spiders also have simple eyes that have only one lens.

Drone
A male bee. Drones mate with the queen bee and do not join in the work of the colony.

Elytra
The hardened front wings of insects such as beetles that fold over and protect the back wings. Elytra are not used for flight.

Fangs
Pointed mouthparts, some of which inject venom into prey.

Fungi (*singular,* fungus)
Simple living things that are not green plants and not animals. Mushrooms and toadstools are examples of fungi.

Gland
A part of the body that produces special substances, such as enzymes and poisons, which are passed to the outside of the body or into the blood. A gland in a scorpion, for example, makes the venom that it injects into its victim when it stings.

Halteres
A pair of small, knobbed structures, one on each side of a fly's body. Halteres help the fly to maintain balance during flight.

Host
An animal on or in which a parasite lives and feeds.

Larvae (*singular,* larva)
Young insects that look very different from the adult form. A caterpillar, for example, is the larva of a butterfly.

Lichen
A mixture of fungi and simple plants called algae that live on the surface of rocks and trees.

Maggot
The wormlike larva of a fly.

Migration
The movement of creatures from one area to another. Migrations are usually made to find better weather or more food.

Nectar
A sugary liquid (produced by plants) that attracts pollinating insects. While an insect is feeding on nectar, it picks up pollen on its body that it may then take on to the next flower it visits. If this pollen reaches the female part of the plant, then that plant is fertilized and can produce seeds.

Nymph
Larva of insects such as dragonflies and grasshoppers. The nymphs go straight to the adult stage without becoming pupae.

Parasite
A creature that lives and feeds on or inside another living creature. Fleas are parasites. They live in the fur of other animals such as cats and dogs (their hosts) and feed on their blood.

Pollen
Tiny grains made by the male parts of a flower. Pollen must reach the female parts of a flower so that seeds can form. Pollen is often carried between one flower and another by insects such as bees, wasps, and flies.

Pupae (*singular,* pupa)
The pupa is the stage in the lives of some kinds of insects when they change from larvae to adults. Usually during the pupal stage the insect is encased in some sort of protective covering such as a cocoon and does not move.

Saliva
A colorless liquid made in the mouth by glands. Insects use saliva to help them digest their food and to mix with soil when they build nests.

Social
Social insects are those that live in huge groups. They include ants, bees, wasps, and termites.

Species
A particular type of animal or plant. Members of the same species can mate and produce young that can have young themselves. Members of one species do not mate with members of another species.

Spinnerets
The fine tubes at the end of a spider's abdomen. Silk for spinning a web comes out of the spider's body through the spinnerets.

Stinger
The sharp part of an insect or scorpion with which it delivers its sting.

Thorax
The second part of an insect's body, between the head and the abdomen. An insect's legs are attached to the thorax.

Venom
A liquid made by an animal that is used to kill or paralyze prey. The stinger at the end of a scorpion's "tail" injects venom.

Workers
Those insects in a social colony that do all the work—building the nest, finding food, and caring for young. There are worker bees, ants, and termites.

INDEX